QUESTIONS ABOUT WISDOM AND LOVE

Some important questions for myself

Copyright © 2009	Bengt Rudqvist
ISBN	978-1-84409-172-0
Publisher	Findhorn Press
	305a The Park, Findhorn,
	Forres IV36 3TE, Scotland, UK
	+44(0)1309 690582
	info@findhornpress.com
	www.findhornpress.com
Photo and text	Bengt Rudqvist
Visual editing	Photographer Tom Bengtsson
	Visual Artist Du Mats
Layout	Pia Yngveson & Jonas Ahlgren
Production leader	Per-Ingvar Skoglund
Printed in	China
Original title	Frågor kring visdom & kärlek
English translation	Maria Trap
Edited by	Jane Engel

QUESTIONS ABOUT WISDOM AND LOVE

Some important questions for myself

Bengt Rudqvist

FINDHORN PRESS

To Magnus, Martin and Monica

you helped me out of
my deepest, utmost pain…
…towards highest Love

Contents

Foreword..........................8

Guidelines for reading.............12

THE FIRST STEPS

- To think and to have feelings.......15
- To create a meaningless or a meaningful world................17
- To show discontent or happiness....18

THE WILL TO CHANGE

- To see in a different way...........21
- To attack or to understand.........25
- To forgive.........................26
- To see problems and to find solutions..........................29

DEVELOPMENT

- To give and to receive.............31
- To defend or to be free from defensiveness............32
- To judge and to forgive............35

MY CHOICES

- To get to know myself; Who am I? What am I?.............37
- To make important choices.........39

TOWARDS A NEW REALITY

- To give importance to the present..41
- To give and to receive the gifts of acceptance and re-union...........42
- To live in love....................45

COMPLETION

- Love.............................47

Bibliography......................55

Foreword

Life can seem unreal at times. Sometimes it feels as if you have made an unnecessary journey to a place that did not even exist. And yet, you have met so many fascinating people and situations on the way...

Sometimes experiences seem almost surrealistic or hard to believe but natural at the same time. Often unforeseen things happen to me, things that I never could have thought out beforehand and while they are often called 'coincidences' I have started to doubt that because they happen so often.

During the years I have asked myself many questions about life such as: "Who am I?" "What is the meaning of life?" "How do I think?" These types of questions have become central for me and they form the main theme of this book. I have given myself different answers through the years and therefore I no longer think that there is just one answer. For the same reason it has become important for me to keep these questions alive and see how the answers shift. The many questions posed in this book are my own questions to myself and I am still asking them.

My inner development really took off after we had two children. Those were big events that gradually changed me. From having been alone I then developed towards a unit, towards a family. This inner development was reinforced by meditation that I started in order to learn to listen inwards and by reading psychological and philosophical literature.

During this time I also read *A Course in Miracles*, a book of about 1400 pages with timeless philosophical, psychological and spiritual wisdom. It suggests that there are other ways to think and to look at the world. It is about big subjects that challenge us to examine our thoughts, feelings and choices: to understand our anger and pain, discontent and happiness, to learn forgiveness and re-union, to give and receive love and to find peace. The book has become a source of wisdom for millions of readers all over the world and has continued to inspire me for many years.

As I read the Course in English, I formulated my own personal questions in Swedish, my mother tongue, based on the provocative and

Foreword

supporting texts. I found it was easier for me to work more with them in that way, and to try to understand them on a deeper level.

I wrote the first, Swedish version of *Questions about Wisdom and Love* in 2004 in order to share my way of translating some inspiring parts of *A Course in Miracles* into my own personal questions. It contained a selection of my questions that are mainly about how I as a human being think, feel and choose. The many positive responses of Swedish readers made me take the step to have the book translated in English, so that it can be shared with a much wider circle of readers.

Everyone has to find his or her own answers and they may be all different and will vary over time. If this book inspires readers to look for answers within themselves and to make their own journey of discovery, I'll be very happy.

Over the years many people have inspired and supported me through personal conversations in which they have shared their own questions and experiences. Some have become like mentors to me and others have become friends for life.

First of all I want to thank Carl Rogers who over a period of five years was my first psychological guide on my journey. Then, that journey became more of a philosophical nature under Peter Koestenbaums guidance for about ten years. Through all these years Jan Backelin has been invaluable as my speaking partner. He tirelessly and generously shared his insights in the countless creative conversations we had.

Several other people have inspired me through personal meetings and also through their books. Those with English titles are mentioned in the Bibliography.

In addition I would like to mention some organizations that have been important to me: These include the internationally-known Findhorn Foundation in Scotland; and Organization Transformation (OT); and two Swedish organizations: Living Companies

Foreword

(Levande Företag) and Nourishment & Life (Näring & Liv). Through all these I have met many people at conferences, seminars and workshops who have given me energy, ideas and happiness on my journey.

Last and surely not least, I want to thank my family and our close friends, who have given me so much encouragement and love over the years, especially when things felt difficult and heavy.

Falkenberg
August 2008
Bengt Rudqvist

Foreword

GUIDELINES FOR READING

This book is not intended to be read the way you would normally read a book. It can be used as a resource in various ways and I would suggest the following:

1. Think of someone/something that has been or is important to you in your relationships. This could be regarding your partner, children or parents, yourself, another person in your life or a certain situation.

2. Ask yourself a question about this relationship/situation that feels important.

3. Next open the book at random and point at or let your eyes rest on a short piece of text on that page.

4. Then reflect: Does the question/statement in this piece give you an answer? Does the text you chose give new meaning to your question or does it suggest that you reframe it? Do various associations and connections with your question come up and give you your own 'oracle answer'?

This kind of inner dialogue can result in surprising new thoughts, feelings and insights.

I have found that to get most benefit from the book, it is best to only read and work with short pieces while taking time to quietly reflect on them. This way you can let the different feelings and thoughts come up. I suggest you give yourself some time to let them sink in. The reflections on your own associations and answers as well as on your own questions will vary depending on your feelings and circumstances, so don't hesitate to ask yourself the same question several times.

Another way to work with the book is to answer every question in the book with a simple yes/no/don't know or with just a few words that you formulate yourself. This process can also give you an interesting overall picture of yourself and your attitude towards life.

Guidelines for reading

I forgive my self...
for having misunderstood
almost everything...

The first steps

The first steps

TO THINK AND
TO HAVE FEELINGS

Imagine that it is true that...

...everything I see, experience and feel actually only reflects my own thought patterns?

... nothing that I experience in a situation or a relationship means anything in and of itself? Instead is it my own attitude towards what I experience that is the important factor?

...my thoughts, that I create myself, give me all my meaning in life and generate all my choices?

...my thoughts and feelings are connected with something outside of that which exists in the present? Perhaps something that comes from good and bad experiences in the past, or from fantasies about what could happen in the future, can affect my thoughts and feelings?

Maybe my brain is mostly occupied with previous experiences and tries to remember something from the past, for which it already has models and habitual patterns?

If I mainly see the past in everything or fantasise about the future, will I then be able to experience reality as it is here and now?

The first steps

TO CREATE A MEANINGLESS OR A MEANINGFUL WORLD

Do I experience worry, emptiness and loneliness when I perceive my world as meaningless?

Do I experience happiness and connectedness when I perceive my world as meaningful?

Does my experience show me that…

…I myself create either a meaningful or a meaningless world through my own thoughts, feelings, attitudes and my own will?

…in many situations I do not understand what is best for me? Are my desires often contradictory or unclear? Do I often have unclear visions and goals?

…I am not alone in experiencing the effects of my feelings and thoughts? Do they lead to words and deeds from me that I am responsible for? Do they also affect and influence others?

…that I do not have neutral thoughts? Does every thought contribute either to something positive or something negative, to something true or something false, to something real or to something illusionary?

The first steps

TO SHOW DISCONTENT OR HAPPINESS

Does my discontent and my complaining keep me from experiencing happiness?

Does discontent and complaining create guilt feelings in me?

Do happiness and love ever contain discontent and complaints?

Is it true that…

…if I feel discontent, guilt or other negative feelings, I myself can influence and change these feelings through my thoughts?

…if I see the cause of my discontent in the outer world, that in order for me to become happy, I must either change my picture of the world or the circumstances in the world need to change?

..if I see the cause of my discontent in my own attitudes and in my way of thinking, I can change these attitudes and set myself free?

Can I let possibilities, happiness and clarity replace complaining and discontent?

Is my picture of the world really a mirror image of my own thinking?

Can I, through my own will and thoughts, create and develop peace and happiness in my inner world?

The first steps

The will to change

The will to change

TO SEE IN A DIFFERENT WAY

Which of the following standpoints are important to me if I want to change my way of thinking?

- I am determined to learn to see reality as it is.

- I decide to question my previous knowledge and prejudices about what everything is and what meaning it has. I try then to be open to learning new things.

- I have a choice to see there are different ways to look at every problem and every situation.

- I do not want to be a victim and I am not a victim of the world that I see.

- I am not a victim of anything other than my own way of thinking and feeling and of the attitudes I myself consciously or unconsciously choose.

The will to change

- I create my own experience of every situation that I find myself in. I am responsible for my own way of looking at every situation.

- I can try to replace my negative feelings of fear, anger etc. with thoughts of peace and happiness.
  I have my free will; I have the power to create and to choose.

- I have my free will and I have the power to choose.

- I already have an underlying knowing about good and evil, trust and worry, love and fear, for divine and the worldly; with experience I can develop this further.

- I can always try to stand firm against my being negative and I can try to act for the good.

- I know that clarity, to see reality as it is, is life's challenge.

- Most of my deepest thoughts are related to the emotional opposites of love / fear and separation / re-union.

The will to change

The will to change

TO ATTACK OR TO UNDERSTAND

Is it true that...

...I sometimes experience others as attacking me or taking revenge on me? Do I also attack others sometimes or take revenge on others? Do I mostly experience my own attack as defense?

...my thoughts, when I attack others, also often hurt myself?

...nothing other than my own feelings and thoughts about my experiences can hurt me? Do I have many thoughts, feelings and behaviours that actually are attacks on myself?

...I can lose my negative patterns of behaviour and put an end to my attacking thoughts and actions through forgiving myself and others instead?

...nothing other than my own thoughts and feelings can get me to understand that I feel vulnerable, afraid and alone?

Can I instead think about my own strengths (such as trust, love and happiness) so that I can try to understand, forgive and love myself and others?

Can I support my own development and learning?

TO FORGIVE

What if it is true that...

...forgiveness is learning to make up and to become re-connected?

...forgiveness, making up and re-connecting give freedom and happiness?

...forgiving and re-connecting is like saying to yourself: I am not going to let myself feel self-pity, isolation and needing others to like me through pitying me? Am I willing to instead see my own part of the problems and to change what I have done wrong?

...behind every enemy, after I have forgiven and re-connected with him, there is a good friend?

...I can forgive myself and my own inner picture of the world? Can I then create a new inner world and a new future for myself?

The will to change

The will to change

TO SEE PROBLEMS AND TO FIND SOLUTIONS

Do problems and solutions occur simultaneously if I stop, think and use my creativity?

Do solutions to problems come to me when I understand and forgive my own and others' misinterpretations and misunderstandings about both the matter itself and the way it came about?

Is there one main problem behind everything – separation – but disguised in a million different forms?

Is re-connection often the one main solution for everything – but which can be disguised in a million different ways?

Which of the following standpoints are helpful when choosing solutions?

- There are only two alternatives to choose from, however many there may seem to be!
- It's a matter of choosing all or nothing!
- In taking away from others I also take away from myself!
- What is the goal? What is this action meant to achieve? What attracts me?

If I feel worry, guilt or other negative feelings inside myself then the choice is wrong!

When I feel happiness, harmony and other positive feelings inside myself then the choice is right!

Development

Development

TO GIVE AND
TO RECEIVE

Is it perhaps true that…

…when I help others, I actually also help myself?

…what I give to others, on some level I also give to myself?

…what I do towards others, on some level I also do to myself?

Is the saying "As I sow so shall I reap" true?

…on a deeper level, to give and to receive is actually the same thing?

…maybe I don't understand who I am and what I have inside me until I share of myself with others?

TO DEFEND OR TO BE FREE FROM DEFENSIVENESS

If I defend myself when I feel attacked, do I then actually attack others?

Does defensiveness come from fear – for example the fear of separation, ridicule or becoming crazy?
Does the fear increase after every "defense" because it feels as if there will be another attack coming?

Does my strength lie in my freedom from my defenselessness and my openness?
Is that my real and best defense?

Development

Development

TO JUDGE AND TO FORGIVE

Imagine that it is true that...

...my misinterpretations and misunderstandings form the basis for my mistakes?

...my judgment of others and of myself is deep down actually hurting me?

...my forgiving and accepting of what is ends most of my suffering and worrying?

... my forgiving and accepting of what is forms the key to my own liberation and my own peace?

...when I try to understand, forgive and accept what is, I then see the situation differently?

Am I trying to understand forgiveness for what it really is: acceptance and re-union?

Do understanding, forgiving and re-union give me what, deep down, I want to have most?

Can I today abstain from judging or guessing what will happen?

My choices

My choices

TO GET TO KNOW MYSELF: WHO AM I? WHAT AM I?

Is it true that...

...I have a body, but I am not just that body? Do I also have a consciousness, a will and a self?

...I can see another not only as a body, but also as a consciousness, a will and a self, that can be connected with my own consciousness, will and self?

...the ability and the power to want, choose and decide really are my own?

...my own liberation is dependent upon my own decisions?

...I always can learn something from every situation?

Do I want to be at peace or do I want to be right?

Can the desire for peace and the desire for truth go together hand in hand?

My choices

TO MAKE IMPORTANT CHOICES

Which of the following choices can and do I want to make through my own will?

- I choose to change all thoughts that I think hurt me!

- I choose to fully accept myself as I am!

- I choose to discover my illusions…and then give them up!

- I choose to give up my fear and feel that I am safe!

- I choose to speak my truth and to respect others!

- I choose to see myself as unlimited and full of possibilities!

- I choose to trust myself and to create connectedness, community and cooperation with others!

Do I realize that I can free myself from all destructive feelings and thoughts?

Can I live in love, freedom and happiness instead of in fear, constraint and worry through the choices I make for myself?

Towards a new reality

Towards a new reality

TO GIVE IMPORTANCE TO THE PRESENT

Can I downplay and make peace with my own past and the pasts of others?

Is the past over? Can it not affect me even if I do not want it to?

Is this moment – right now – the most important time there is?

Can I make this 'now' into a moment of stillness and peace?

TO GIVE AND TO RECEIVE THE GIFTS OF ACCEPTANCE AND RE-UNION

Are all gifts that other people give me, also given to themselves?

Are all gifts that I give to other people, also given to myself?

Does my fear and anxiety keep me bound to my own world?

Does my forgiveness and acceptance of what is set me free?

Does my forgiveness, acceptance and re-union put an end to all my conflicts and give me peace?

Are forgiveness, acceptance and re-union the most important gifts I have to offer?

Today, can I try to embrace all things with forgiveness and total acceptance, so that I myself am also embraced by forgiveness and total acceptance?

Towards a new reality

Towards a new reality

TO LIVE IN LOVE

Do anger, fear and discontent come from judging?

   Is judgement the weapon that I use towards others and myself?

   Is judgement the opposite of love?

   Is negative behaviour the result of my misunderstandings, misconceptions and my faulty thinking? Does this lead to fear and other negative feelings that are the opposite of love?

   When all fear is gone, is only love and trust left?

Towards a new reality

I love my self…
from the beginning of time…
…'till eternity

Completion

LOVE

Love includes
    the cosmic in the earthly,
    the spiritual in the human,
    all of you in all of me,
    the consciousness of the self
    in my personal consciousness,
    the constant miracles
    in my most inner self.

Love contains
    all that's in my inner cosmos and
    all that is in my outer cosmos,
    all my giving and my receiving,
    all that always is alive in me and
    all that is constantly being reborn.

Completion

*Love embraces the contact,
cooperation and re-union...*

of the cosmic in the earthly,
    because the self is created by love
    present in everything we do,

of the spiritual in the human
    because we – our inner selves
    – are all created
    in the image of love,
    all alike in earthly love and acceptance,
    freedom and responsibility,
    creativity and creative power,

of all of you in all of me,
    because we are all love's children and
    each other's sisters and brothers and
    our essence is still the same
    as the Love that created us,

*of the consciousness of self in my personal
consciousness,*
    because everything comes
    from the same source,
    from incomprehensible love,
    will and thought,
    that becomes our conscious love,
    will and thought,
    that forms the basis for our action
    in the world,

of the constant miracles in my most inner self,
    because lifegiving love
    is always working inside me,
    in the inner space where loving grace meets
    human misunderstandings and mistakes.

Completion

Completion

Completion

Love is always working in me...

*through everything in my inner cosmos and
everything in my outer cosmos,*
    because they mirror each other,
    based upon the images of
    God, the world and myself
    that I chose to create,

through all my giving and all my receiving,
    because what I give to others,
    I also give to myself somehow,
    and what I receive from others,
    they also can receive themselves.
    It is only when I give and receive
    that I really understand who I am myself,

*through all that is constantly alive in me and
everything that is continuously being reborn,*
    because everything inside me is
    pulsating energy,
    the flow of the self.
    There is no death of the self,
    only different forms of energy.
    I choose to surrender to the Self.

Completion

Love surrounds life through
the pulsating energy,
the understanding, forgiveness, acceptance
and re-unification of the miracles inside me.

Love is the foundation,
developed in existence,
in stillness is cleansed and refined,
through the body and the senses,
through awareness and feelings,
through the Will and the Self.

Completion

Love
perceived by feeling – the partly subconscious,
developed by thought – the conscious,
chosen by will – the sublime,
inspired by miracles - the eternal,
expressed in words and
shown in actions.

Gravity is the root of lightness and
stillness the father of movement,
silence is the source of hearing and
light is the mother of life.
Love is the seeing of clarity.
Love is the clarity of seeing.

Bibliography

Bibliography

Below is a list of English language books, the authors of which have been of major importance in my life, often through meetings in person as well as through their writings. Several Swedish titles I have left out. Besides these I have read hundreds of interesting books and articles, the authors of which I unfortunately have never met.

Bibliography

Eileen Caddy
-God Spoke to Me

Dalai Lama
-The Art of Happiness

David Gerson & Gail Straub
-Empowerment: The Art of Creating Your Life as You Want it

Willis W. Harman
-An Incomplete Guide to the Future

Jack Hawley & John A. Hawley
-Reawakening the Spirit in Work: The Power of Dharmic Management

Peter Koestenbaum
-Managing Anxiety
-Is there an Answer to Death?
-The New Image of the Person
-Philosophy in Business

Elisabeth Kübler-Ross & Heather Preston
Remember the Secret

George Leonard
The Silent Pulse: A Search for the Rhythm that Exists in Each of Us

Rollo May
-Love and Will
-The Cry for Myth
-The Discovery of Being: Writings in Existential Psychology

Carl Rogers
-On Becoming a Person
-Becoming Partners
-Client-centred Therapy
-Carl Rogers on Encounter Groups
-Freedom to learn

Natalie Rogers
-Emerging Woman: A Decade of Midlife Transitions

Sabina A. Spencer & John D. Adams
-Reflections
-Life Changes: A Guide to the Seven Stages of Personal Growth

Frances E. Vaughan
-Awakening Intuition

Frances E. Vaughan & Roger Walsh
-A Gift of Peace
-Accept this Gift

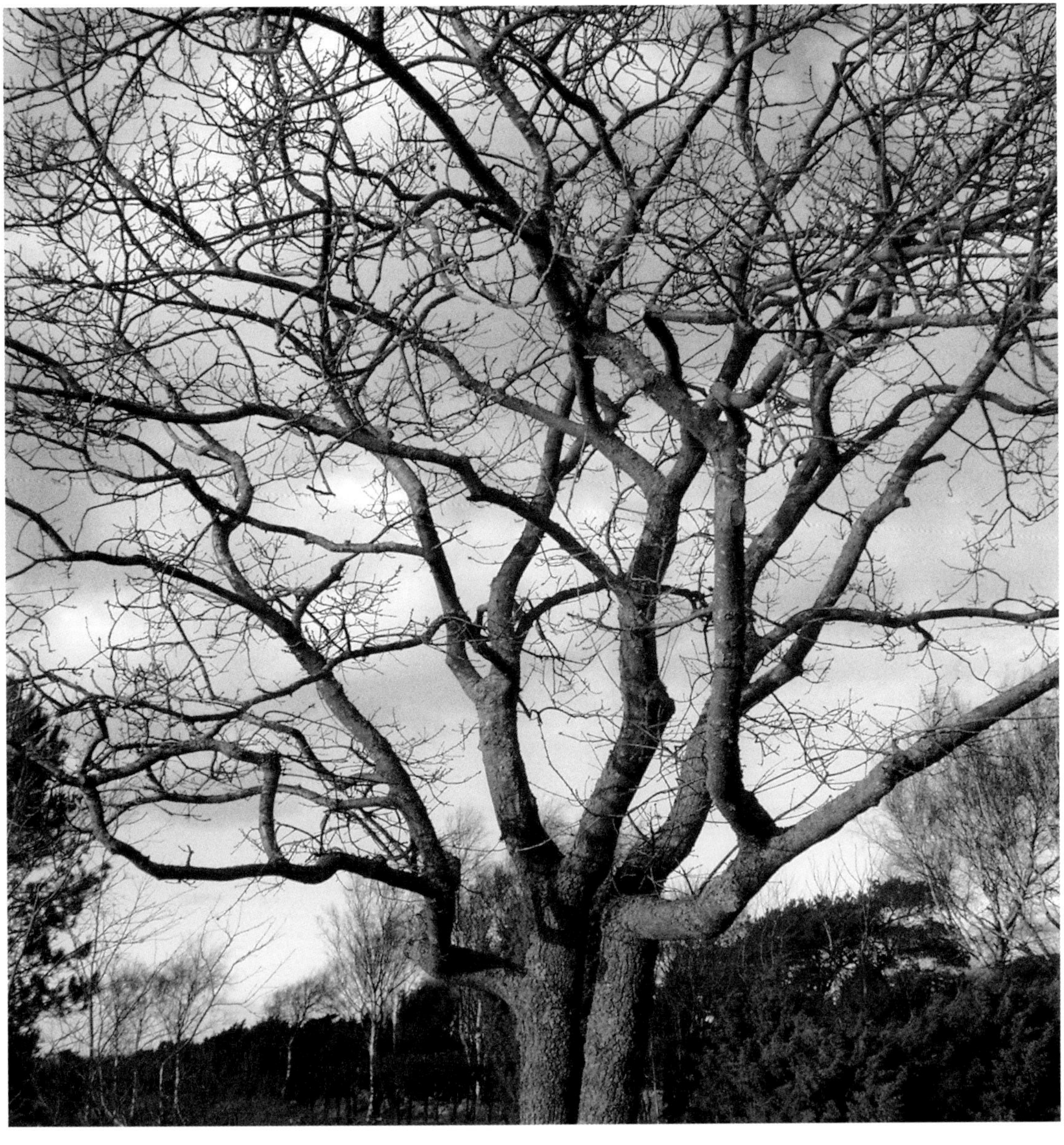

Before important decisions:
What is the actual vision and motivation
behind what I want to do?
Go inside and listen!

FINDHORN PRESS

Life Changing Books

For a complete catalogue,
please contact:

Findhorn Press
305a The Park, Findhorn
Forres IV36 3TE
Scotland, UK

t +44(0)1309 690582
f +44(0)131 777 2711
e info@findhornpress.com

or consult our catalogue online
(with secure order facility) on
www.findhornpress.com

For information on the Findhorn Foundation Community:
www.findhorn.org